Free/Inexpensive Ways To Create Passive Income:

How To Make $25,000 Each Month On Autopilot For The Millionaire In Progress

By Carlos Bermudez

Copyright © 2018

Carlos Bermudez

All Rights Reserved

Disclaimer:

All attempts have been made to verify the information in this book; however, neither the author nor the publisher assumes any responsibility for errors, omissions, or contrary interpretations of the content within.

This book is for entertainment purposes only, and so the views of the author should not be taken as expert instruction or commands. The reader is responsible for his or her own actions.

Adherence to all applicable laws, including but not limited to international, federal, state, and local regulations governing professional licensing, business practices, advertising, and all other aspects of doing business in the United States or any other jurisdiction is the sole responsibility of the purchaser or reader.

Neither the author nor the publisher assumes any responsibility or liability on behalf of the purchaser or reader of this book.

Table of Contents

1. Who This Book Is For
2. Green Machine
3. Passive Income Ideas That Seem Great... On Paper
4. Affiliate Marketing: A Great Foundation
5. eBooks/Paperbacks
6. Blogging
7. ATM Business
8. Creating An Online Training Course/Program To Sell
9. YouTube
10. Patience Is Key
11. Do Me Favor

Other Books

Who This Book Is For

We all know having a little extra cash in our wallet would be very beneficial. There's just so much we could do with it if. Now, imagine making enough passive income to the point where you would be able to quit your nine to five job and spend all of your free time doing whatever it is you wanted. The amazing thing about that is that it's already being done every day by people like you and me! They've already cracked the code. But, how? There are many people today talking about creating passive income, but most of us don't know how to actually do it whether it be short term or in the long run. We've heard millionaires talking about it. We've heard college dropouts talking about it. We've all seen the promoted advertisements on the internet. Yet, how do you actually do it?

If you're like me I'm sure you've already surfed the web, using Google, to search for the answers. That's actually how it all started for me. I was tired of working nine to five jobs. I was tired of all the stress and drama that was associated with the line of work I had. All I wanted to do was leave, but I couldn't. Want to know why? I wanted to leave because I wasn't being paid as much I'm worth but was being paid just enough to keep crawling back to my job every morning. It's a paradox. I had bills to pay and was too afraid to just leave. So, I decided to search the web after I too had come across many paid advertisements on Facebook.

After hours of searching, the only options I could find were generic ones. For example, real estate house flipping and investing in the stock market. I'm sure those are great ways to make passive income if you really know what it is you're doing, and I'm sure if I took the time to really study them I could learn it all, but the real problem was that I was lacking the funds to even start. Most of the ideas on the internet today are all focused around having large sums of disposable cash in the beginning, and yet most of us don't have any disposable cash in the first place! All we have are ambitions and the dedication to work for it!

But worry not. There is hope. I want you to think about something for just a minute. Imagine yourself generating enough passive income to the point of becoming financially free. Whether that's $3,000 a month or $30,000 a month. Imagine yourself finally being able to quit your nine to five job and having all that free time to spend it with the people you love most. No longer will you be paid less than you are worth, but enough to keep crawling back to your job. No longer will you settle for less than you deserve. You deserve to enjoy everything life has to offer and the only way to do so is to earn it. It is your responsibility to learn how to create passive income in order to multiply your money. This may sound difficult at first, but by investing a little bit of cash and some of your time, you'll be able to create a passive income generating machine in no time.

Green Machine

It's the next morning and the alarm clock on your phone wakes you up. The first thing you do is check your phone to see all the notifications you've received over night. Once you've cleared them out, you then decide to check your bank account. When you log in, you see a bit over $4,000 dollars has been deposited into your account since your last payment two weeks ago. How great does that sound? What if you could check your phone every morning and see that you've made money without actively doing anything? I'm talking about making $600 to $5,000+ per month in the next three months. What if you could work on something once and reap the benefits month after month? Sounds too good to be true? Well, it's not. Stop being cynical. The reality is this is being done every single day by all walks of people. College students, college dropouts, people with MBA degrees, nurses, busy stay at home mothers or fathers. Day in and day out, people are making more and more money by simply investing their time into creating a passive income generator. In essence, you are creating a business that runs on autopilot to generate passive income for you. I want you to imagine that for a moment. Do you really think this is possible? Am I just bullshiting you? I'm not. I've already accomplished this. Now it's your turn.

But before we get started, I have to make sure you believe what I'm telling you. I have to make sure you believe in yourself first. So many people want to become financially free yet don't believe it is possible to do so. I understand there are many people in your life currently bringing you down and telling you it's not possible, but don't listen to them. They're cynics. If people believe they can't do something, they'll make sure to make you believe you can't do it either. Don't listen to them. You can do it. There's proof everywhere that it is possible. All you have to do is desire it. Constantly self-affirm yourself that it is possible. Constantly imagine yourself generating enough wealth to become financially free.

I mean, think about how different your life would be if you didn't have to work for your money anymore? Think about not having to go back to that dead-end job? No more bosses. No more deadlines. No more daily commute. No more fear of not having enough money at the end of the month to pay your bills. Because generating passive income usually means earning money off a product, book royalties, rental/dividend income from real estate properties, sub charges, or ads, it also means you'll be dealing with people less. No more selling, pitching, or presenting to your potential clients. No more having to deal with angry customers. No more having to recruit, hire, or manage employees. Just pure profit from the product/investment that sells itself. That's the beauty of building ways to create passive income. Now, there are so many ways out there to earn passive income and there are a lot of books/articles that list out all the ways you can earn passive income, but they're all either very generic or very expensive. Worst of all, they don't list any of the steps you'll need to take.

In this book I will be discussing non-expensive ways of creating passive income and I will be teaching you, step by step, how to go about building them. Some of them are as easy as doing some research, but others will require a bit more work and dedication. I will be showing you exactly how I was able to create an empire of passive income by simply incorporating and implementing these methods. This book will be fast, simple, and to the point. If you follow every step that I've laid out for you and stay focused, you can go from making zero to making thousands of dollars every month relatively quickly.

Here's the catch though. Unlike actively working for your money with a job, this will require you to be very patient. Remember, Rome wasn't built in one day.

Passive Income Ideas That Seem Great... On Paper.

Like I've already mentioned, there are a lot of generic articles online, and even books on Amazon that talk about making passive income. A lot of the most popular books being sold on Amazon are very generic, high-leveled, and lack a detailed step by step plan. Although a lot of the ideas and options that are given may be good ones, they usually require a large initial capital investment of $10,000 or more. That may not be a lot of money in the grand scheme of things, but that is a lot more money than most people want to put down or have when they're starting off. If you're like me, you want to be able to start investing your time into great ideas that will create the best forms of passive income. I mean, that's why you bought this book, right? Exactly. And that's why I wrote it.

I recommend to look at this as a business and not a game. I repeat, passive income is not a game nor is it a scam, it's a business. Because it is a business, it's going to take some proper planning, work, and time. There is a high level of commitment here and you must be willing to uphold it. That said, there are many different ways you can make passive income now-a-days, but I don't recommend all of them. Why you may ask? Some of them cost too much money and can cost upwards of fifty thousand dollars liquidity to begin. Some of them take way too many years before yielding anywhere close to passive income. And if you're still a beginner working a full-time job, then odds are you won't have much of either to spare. So, before I get into the best and inexpensive ways for creating passive income, let's go over some of the passive income ideas that I don't recommend and their cons:

- **<u>Multi-Level Marketing (a.k.a. Pyramid Scheme):</u>**

I was once involved in a multi-level marketing company because I was introduced to, and recruited by, a man making around seven thousand dollars every month doing it. The man showed me how much he was making per month and asked me if I wanted to join the company so that I could also be pulling in the same type of money every month. I was new to the idea of passive income, so of course I said yes. The company focused around trading currencies with FOREX and offered a learning platform to their members. The platform gave you access to multiple educational videos taught by the owner of the

17

company and focused on learning how to make money by trading. On the flip side, the other way one could make money was by recruiting people to work under you. With every person that you recruited, a certain dollar amount would be paid to you every month by the company. Every week or so there would also be a nationwide video-call from some of the top players making well over eight figures. We were then told to invite our friends and family to hop onto the call in order to use the video as leverage to persuade them to join the company and have them work under us. In doing so, our brackets would grow larger and increase our monthly payment.

<u>Verdict:</u>

I really didn't make much money trading FOREX. In fact, I actually lost well over a grand. And although I did have a decent size bracket of people under me, I really didn't make much money in the five months I was in it. What I did learn was that if you're good with people, are very aggressive at selling yourself, are willing to follow the company's system, and invest your time and money into their training events, you can make some decent money. In the end I was actually happy to leave and get out of the MLM. The people that really utilize the company's system to recruit two people per day are the only ones that truly make any sort of money. The hardest part about an MLM is not recruiting, but rather keeping your recruits. You have to constantly preach and make them believe that what they are involved in is a worthy cause and all they have to do is simply follow the system to recruit others the same way they themselves were recruited. Again, not only will you have to sell yourself and the product, you have to convince other people to start selling the product and recruiting others too. That just wasn't for me.

- **E-Commerce Stores and Online Drop Shipping:**

E-Commerce refers to the process of selling products online. For example, eBay, Shopify, Amazon, etc. E-commerce requires a lot of time and effort in the beginning to launch correctly. You'll first need to find a reliable supplier. Most of the time the one supplier that people go with are Chinese ones because they are the cheapest to use. Next, you'll need to create a good-looking website and you'll also need to purchase a domain. Once you've done that, you'll need to pick products to sell, create good looking listings, and publish your online store. Lastly, you'll have to invest in internet ads to get some traffic on your site. Once you have the business going, you can pretty much sit back and collect your earnings every month. It's a great way to make passive income actually. Some of the people doing drop shipping make well over $100,000 per month!

Verdict:

You can make really good money with an e-commerce store, especially if you're selling a hot product, but that isn't always the hardest part. Yes, you'll have to do some studying to figure out what is popular and selling like hot buns right now, but you'll also have to learn marketing. Not only will you have to invest considerable amounts of money into your advertising, you'll actually have to learn how to properly do them! I'm talking about SEO, AdWords, Facebook Ads Manager, social media marketing and advertising, Split-testing, etc. These can take months to learn how to really use them properly and make them work to your advantage.

- **Real Estate Investing:**

One of the best and most sure ways of creating high profits is by investing in real estate. In fact, through recorded history, real estate has created the most millionaires in the United States. There's a good reason behind it, too. Know why? Well, there's an old saying that goes, "Invest in real estate. God isn't making any more land on this planet." Think about it. People are always going to need somewhere to live. Especially now that the population has grown so big and will only continue to grow astronomically. The most common way to invest in real estate is by purchasing a property, remodeling it/fixing it up, and then sell it for a profit. This particular tactic is called "Flipping" a house or property. This is a great way to make good profit seeing as how by flipping one house, you could make upwards of $60,000 in profits!

Verdict:

Obviously, there is a high barrier of entry, as even properties in an awful state of disrepair will still cost you a lot of money upfront. You will really have to know what you are doing before even thinking about purchasing a house with the intentions of flipping it. You'll have to be good at appraising the house, have certain carpentry skills, and a lot of cash in order to proceed. Sure, you may be able to outsource a lot of this, but again, that will cost you some money upfront. You can make a lot of money doing this, but it does take a lot of time, money, and expertise to become really good at it. AND, above all, this type of real estate isn't really passive income in my opinion. This isn't something you can do once and continuously receive income over the course of your life and that's why I don't consider it to be passive income.

- **High Yielding Savings Account:**

One of the easiest ways to invest/save your money is by depositing it into a "high" yielding savings account.

What this account does for you is every year you will receive a certain percentage of money back into your account for simply having your money in it in the first place. This is commonly known as interest. The amount of money you'll receive from the bank all depends on how much money you've invested into the account, and how high your APY is (Annual Percentage Yield, or Interest). The good news is there are some banks out there that offer these types of accounts at 1% APY, or really close to 1%.

Verdict:

If you save your money, save to invest. Don't just save your money and have it sit there in an account. The average APY (annual percentage yield, or interest) of a savings account is only 0.06%. Think about that. If you had a single dollar in that savings account, every year you'd be gaining six cents in interest. That's not a whole lot. Yes, there are some saving accounts out there that offer closer to 1%, if not 1%, but the truth is your money will never grow as fast as you need it to out run inflation. This may create passive income, but the ROI (Return On Investment) will be too low to really be able to do anything with.

- **Membership Sites:**

The idea behind membership sites is to create a website that offers great free content, but also offers better more exclusive content to its premium members. You have to convince your visitors, by your free content, that it is worth paying a monthly subscription in order to join the ranks of a premium member. This can be done by offering access to special functions to premium members only, special guides, articles, news, videos, entertainment, etc. In order to continue receiving all your valuable content, they will have to continue to pay your monthly subscription fee. You see this a lot with content creators and groups around the internet like Facebook. They usually offer subscriptions to their online marketing, online dating, fat loss program, and other topics of interest to the public.

Verdict:

This works and is a great way to make passive income, but typically it works for those that have already established themselves as experts, be it through their blog, email list, or via through their large content following. Membership sites are not recommended to those that are just starting out with no audience or track record.

- **Photography:**

There are plenty of sites out on the internet that allow users to sell their photos to anyone interested in them. So, if you're a skilled photographer, you can build a great passive income by taking quality photos and offering them to the public or businesses. Your photos could be very useful to online businesses looking for great stock photos to be implemented into their website.

Verdict:

Simply put, anyone can pull out their cell phone and take a picture. Before getting into the business of selling your photos, you'll need to invest in a high-quality camera in order to produce some high-quality photos. Some of these cameras can go well into the high hundreds and low thousands of dollars to purchase them. Keep in mind you'll also need good photo editing software to edit your photos. So, if you're not a photographer already, this will be very hard to pull off.

- **Peer To Peer Lending:**

In a nutshell, borrowers ask for money, and lenders decide how likely it is that they will see that money back. A common example is someone who has $6,000 in credit card debt with a twenty percent annual interest rate. This person will then decide to ask the Peer To Peer lending community to lend them $6,000 at eight percent or ten percent interest rate. If an investor with the capital choses to lend them the money, everyone wins in that scenario. With the borrower paying less to their credit card company and the internet lender getting a nice return on their investment, everyone will be happy. Just to be safe, if repayment is unlikely, those lenders charge a high rate of interest to offset that risk. If the borrower is trustworthy, they'll charge a lower rate of interest to win the business from competing banks.

<u>Verdict:</u>

The risk of losing all your money still exists. If you jump to invest in only the high-risk-category loans with double interest rates, you can easily lose all your money, just like any other investment. Don't chase high returns without understanding the risk that comes with it. You could invest as little as $25 in each loan, but you would still need about $3,750 to invest in enough loans so that a few defaults won't destroy your overall return on investment. This also isn't the best way to create passive income quickly enough as this will take years before you begin to raise enough wealth.

- **<u>Airbnb:</u>**

Airbnb has changed the way the world travels since its launch in 2008. The company, which is now valued well into the billions, has helped homeowners across the globe become mini-hoteliers. It has allowed guests to stay overnight in an extra room or take over the entire home for a set period of time. Airbnb is a great way to constantly receive passive income as most of your customers will be paying you to rent out a certain room or home to stay at. Nearly 50 percent of all Airbnb hosts make more than $500 per month. So, how can all Airbnb hosts max out their earning potential? Well, a rental in a good location, well furnished, well photographed, and attended to with great care and customer service can always pull in two to three times the revenue of an unfurnished, long-term rental. So yes, the money is very good.

Verdict:

While running a profitable Airbnb is not rocket science, it's also not a walk in the park. You will work and work hard. Laundry, cleaning, stocking, key handoffs, pre-stay communication, in-stay responses, calendar management, and the occasional repairs are all part and parcel of this venture. There's also the problem with not being surrounded by many tourist attractions. If your home or renting area is not near many tourist attractions and is, let's say in the middle of nowhere, there won't be much traffic in line to book your rental property.

My Final Thoughts

Again, these are all ways one could make passive income or some kind of profit along the way, but they aren't the most ideal for you start off with. People do make money these ways, and I do know some people that are making a lot of money from almost all of these methods, but they take quite a bit of time, specialized knowledge and a significant investment to pull off. For these reasons, I don't think they are the best options to make passive income for beginners, so I would stay away from them unless you are being mentored or are really interested in learning/executing how to go about executing them. In fact, I think eventually you should definitely branch out into many of these methods as they are all good streams of income seeing as how the best way to actually become financially free is by having multiple streams of income. It's too dangerous to just have one source of income, like your everyday nine to five jobs. This goes hand in hand with the popular saying, "Don't put all your eggs in one basket."

Anyways, the goal right now is to learn how to make passive income. We've already discussed the other generic options people have been writing books and posting articles about. Although they are ways of making some money, they are not the best for you at this moment. Now it's time I teach you how to start making your first $100 passively. And believe me when I tell you, once you've earned those $100, you'll be hooked!

You'll have the belief and self-confidence to keep doing it over and over again until your first $100 turns into well over $10,000. Once you master the art of creating passive income, you can start branching out into different ideas than the ones I will be providing for you in this book. Let's get to it, shall we?

Affiliate Marketing: A Great Foundation

I wanted to start off with the method that would build on the rest of the methods in this book. This method is one of the best ones to use in the beginning. You'll understand once you get the ball rolling. Now, what is affiliate marketing? Affiliate marketing is the process of earning a commission by promoting other people's, or companies, products. All you have to do is find a product you like, promote it to others using different methods of advertisement, and earn a piece of the profit for each sale that you make. It's very interesting to note how easy it is to learn how affiliate marketing works, and how you can make money from it. Of course, you will need to invest some time and energy to get started, but that's why you're here! Getting started is not nearly as hard as going to law school or attending an MBA program, which are some of the traditional ways for learning how to make money.

Another Great thing about affiliate marketing is that you do not even need to be a great writer or the ultimate marketing expert to succeed. All you need to do is progress over time, try out different programs, market different products/services, and see which strategies fit your temperament best. What do you stand to gain by engaging in affiliate marketing? If you are looking to make money online, this may be of the best methods to start with and learn. Affiliate marketing is different. With affiliate marketing you don't have to speak with clients directly or be worried about cost of the product or product creation. All you have to do is connect the dots between the buyer and the seller in order to start the money machine flowing. The more dots that are connected the greater amount of income you are potentially able to secure.

The amazing thing about affiliate marketing is that it involves relatively low risk and it doesn't matter if not everyone clicks on the links or purchases the product/service. The reason it doesn't matter is because there is so much traffic available on the internet, what one visitor fails to do, three others will engage with your advertisement successfully. The bottom line is that you don't have to invest a lot of money into affiliate marketing in order for it to work for you. The key here is to have a website, blog, vlog, podcast, YouTube channel, or social media account that is optimized correctly in which you are consistently delivering high-quality content.

Instead of engaging in a separate PPC (Pay Per Click) and SEO (Search Engine Optimization) campaigns, affiliate marketing will help you cut down on costs. That's one of the beauties of it. It's cheap, if not free! The money you would have had to of spent for search engine optimization and/or pay per click campaigns would have been astronomical compared to, let's say, posting an informative YouTube video comparing two products and then asking your viewers to go and purchase the better product. For affiliate marketing to work, the affiliates (You) must create ads to place on their websites, blog, vlog, videos, or accounts. Since you know what kind of visitors and types of audiences will be trafficking through your channels, sites, or accounts, the ads created will be more targeted to that audience in comparison to more generic types of ads.

There are many stories out there of people becoming financially free due to doing affiliate marketing. Just by simply going onto YouTube and searching up success stories, a wide variety of options pop up. In fact, I have a friend of mine racking up some good money every month just by simply doing affiliate marketing on his blog. Now that you understand what affiliate marketing is, and the benefits of it, let's say we get into the process of doing it!

How To Start Affiliate Marketing:

Before you even begin, you'll need to sign up with a company that offers an affiliate program. The most common option, and the one that I recommend, is Amazon's affiliate associate program. Simply go to Google.com and type in the search bar, "Amazon Affiliate Program." Go ahead and click on the first result which will then take you to Amazon's affiliate program website. Once you have arrived, click on the yellow "Join Now For Free" button to get started. After you've clicked on the button, you will either be asked to sign in if you already have an Amazon Prime account, or the website itself will walk you through step by step on completing your application in order to join the program. Once you are ready to go and your account has been approved, you'll then have affiliate commission access to any product on amazon. Simply look up a product and their product link, copy and paste the link into the description of any video, post, or blog, and once people click on it, you could make money by two possible ways. Either the consumer purchases the advertised product and you receive a commission of up to ten percent of the final purchase, or even if the consumer doesn't buy your advertised product but instead purchases anything else off the Amazon website within twenty-four hours, you will receive up to seven percent of the final purchase. This is great because, again, even if they don't buy the product you're advertising and they decide to buy something else then you'll still get a cut of the money! The great thing about Amazon is that they've spent millions and millions of dollars on their algorithm experimenting on their website's optimization to see how they can make more sells. In other words, all you have to do is be convincing and persuasive enough to have the consumer click on the affiliate link and let Amazon's multi-million-dollar sales funnel sell them the product or other products for you. It's great!

Okay, so now that you've signed up for the affiliates program, you will now need decide which niche you're going to target and you'll have to decide which means of communication will work best for you. Are you comfortable in front of a camera and find it easy to convey all your thoughts into words while being recorded? Then building a video blog or, for example a YouTube channel, would be the best option for you! Or, are you more of a writer and have a creative side to you? Then crafting a beautiful website/blog would be the best way for you to start! If you think being in front of a camera isn't the end of the world, then head over to YouTube.com and click "Sign In" in the upper right corner of the screen. Once you've clicked it, I encourage you to sign up with a Gmail account (Google Mail), if you haven't already done so. Once you've signed up for the account, go back to the home page by clicking on the YouTube logo on the upper right-hand side of the screen. Once you are back to the home page, in the upper right-hand side of the screen where the "Sign in" button used to be, there will now be a colored circle with a letter on it. Typically, the letter will be based on your email or the first letter of your name. Go ahead and click on that colored circle. A drop-down menu will then appear and what you'll need to do next is go down to "My Channel" and click on it. This will take you to the section of your channel where you can optimize and customize your YouTube channel. Once you're done with that, click on the video camera icon with the little plus sign in the middle of it in order to upload a video or go live. Once you've clicked on "Upload Video" you will arrive to a screen where you will be given the option to upload a video from your phone or computer. Once you have finished uploading your video, simply add a little bit of text to your description talking about your product or products and leave your affiliate link in the description as well. The key here is to push out as much content directly correlated to product reviews and product comparisons in order to create a successful passive stream of income.

    Personally, I chose to create a website and start a blog because I thought it would be a lot easier for me to do as a beginner than starting a YouTube channel or social media account. Not to say that the other ways aren't the best way, creating a blog was just the most comfortable for me because I was already used to writing. I started building my first site and decided to target people that wanted to become financially free. Seeing as how I had already done it myself, I knew there were many people on the internet trying to find and figure out the answers to becoming financially free themselves. If you don't know what your site is going to be about or who you're going to target with it, you can't really build a site around a product or course that really solves an everyday problem or issue a lot of people have. If you've already figured this one out, way to go! This is undoubtedly one of the most difficult and overwhelming steps. If you don't quite know what your niche is yet, here's some advice that you might find useful. Some key questions to ask yourself when determining your niche are:

- What topics am I already passionate about?

It's much easier to work on something if you're passionate about it. Plus, when you have a passion, you're usually quite knowledgeable about it too, so that definitely helps. For example, if you have a passion about makeup, your niche of choice might be makeup related, too. Or, you might be like me and have an obsession with business and learning how to make money work for you instead of you working for it!

- What do I already have experience in that I could talk about?

This is a great question to ask yourself because it might be the greatest advantage you have. A lot of people don't realize that a lot of their past experiences are ones that can be monetized. Think about the one thing you are most experienced in and the problems that are associated with your experiences. Have you already found solutions to those problems? Great! People that are less experienced are willing to pay for the answers/shortcuts you are willing to provide them with.

- Is there money in this niche?

While following your passion is definitely the recommended option, sometimes the possibility of making money in a profitable niche trumps passion. For example, you may have a passion for underwater basket weaving, but I don't think there is a big enough market for that to take off... You might not necessarily know much about your niche, but if it's likely to make you money, you can always learn more about it. One of the best ways is to do as much research as possible.

Affiliate marketing is a great foundation to know when talking about creating passive income. Because affiliate marketing is so universal, you can easily combine it (trend stack it) with other ideas in order to create beautiful synergy. Yes, that's right. If you combine affiliate marketing with the other ways of creating passive income in this book, it won't be long before the returns will start streaming in from all your efforts combined. This is why I chose to write about this first.

eBooks/Paperbacks

This one is very special to me because this is how I started creating passive income for the first time. As you know, you're reading either a paperback copy of this book, or you're reading the eBook version, so that in itself should tell you that this method works. In fact, writing books is actually one of the best ways for you to start creating passive income. I had seen on the internet that everyday people like you and me were writing books and making anywhere between $5,000 to $30,000 per month just by selling eBooks and paperback copies of their books on Amazon. I thought, "Wow, it sure would be nice to start making that kind of money... but writing a book? Yeesh... That will take forever!" Even though I thought that, I still went on to do a little bit of research on writing eBooks. That's when I came across a specific YouTube video that explained and showed me the exact way to write a book in only a week. Sounds a little unrealistic right? We have been told by others that writing a book usually takes between one to three years to write, so I wasn't sure if I could really write a book in only a week. But like most successful entrepreneurs I was willing to experiment and put in the work.

Since then, I have figured out exactly how to write a book in 7 days for only $7 dollars. Yup, that's right. The total cost for writing a book only costs me a total of $7 dollars and it only takes me seven days to write. Sounds impossible? It's not, and here's how I did it:

How To Write A Book In 7 Days With Only $7.00

Each of us has a unique collection of trials and tough experiences that we've gone through and conquered. The beauty of it is that currently, there are a lot of people that are going through the same trials and experiences that you once went through and are having a hard time figuring out a solution. That said, people are willing to pay you for a short cut or a solution for a specific problem. Your first step is to figure out what past difficult situations in your life have you already figured out? By simply thinking about your life experiences and about all of Life's trials that you have conquered, that will provide you with enough content to write about. That's the secret to making a great selling book; a book that provides the answers to specific adversities. But which markets do you try and sell to? Well, the three markets that will never go out of business are the ones that have to do with Health, Wealth, Love, and Happiness. I recommend taking out a scratch piece of paper and making a list of all the things you've gone through or have a lot of knowledge about.

Once you've created your list, it's time to decide which ones you will be writing about. I recommend starting off with the option that you have the most knowledge and/or experience on seeing as how you won't have to do too much research. After you have chosen which topic to write about, it's time you start outlining the entire book. For this method, what I do every time is write out the three to six main points that I will be writing about. Then, what I'll do is type three sub-points under every main point. Sometimes if there's a lot to write about I'll also include sub-sub-points. I know this all can sound a bit confusing so here's a visual representation of what one of my outlines would look like when preparing to write a book:

Title
Sub-Title

Table of Contents

Introduction

    1. Main Point
- Sub point
- Sub point
- Sub point

    2. Main Point
- Sub point
- Sub point
- Sub point

    3. Main Point
- Sub point
- Sub point
- Sub point
- Sub point

Conclusion

About author

Other Books Written By The Author

The next step after you've completed the outline of your book is to simply begin writing! "But how do you write an entire book in seven days like you said, Carlos?" The key is to write 2,000 words per day. If you do this for seven days straight, your book should have 14,000 words which is a decent length for an eBook seeing as how most eBooks on Amazon today are between 10,000 to 17,000 words long. This may sound easy but I assure you this will take some time to write. Needless to say, make sure you reread and review your work when it's done. People are understanding and will forgive one or two grammatical errors but anything above that makes you look unprofessional.

Once you have completed writing your entire book using the outline, it's time to start thinking about a cover. Here's where the seven dollars come into to play. In my opinion, the best place to get a beautifully done book cover for cheap is on Fivver.com. Fivver is a site where you are able to outsource anything to specialists and experts. Simply go to the search bar and type "eBook and CreateSpace cover." You should now have an endless number of freelancers happily ready take your money for their services. The great thing is most will charge you as little as $5 to create a beautiful cover with unlimited revisions. Keep in mind that you'll typically want to go with someone that is a little more experience, so make sure to search by highest reviews when searching for a freelancer on Fivver.

After you've received your cover, make sure it looks appealing. There's nothing more that will hurt your sales than a tacky looking cover. The books appearance will be a deciding factor in the amount of sales it produces. Next, you'll need to go to Google and type in the search bar "Kindle Direct Publishing." Then, click on the first search result. This will take you to Amazon's direct publishing sight and will prompted up a video in the home page. Go ahead and click on the play button to watch the video. Once you've completed the video, understand that publishing with Amazon is completely FREE! That's right. You won't have to worry about submitting to endless publishers only to get rejected over and over again. Another great thing about self-publishing is that the royalties generated by book sales will be a lot higher than those of normal publishers. Anyways, go ahead and sign up for a kindle direct publishing account.

Once you've filled out your information and completed setting up your account, you'll have to format your book correctly before you upload it. Once you're signed into your KDP account, there should be a section in the middle of the page that gives you the option to either upload your kindle book or upload a paperback version of the book. On the right side of "upload options" there should be four orange bullet points that look like orange circles with check marks on them. Look at the first bullet point that says "Book Content" and click on the link that says "Get started with Kindle content creation tools."

After you've clicked on the link provided, another tab will be open on your screen and you will be taken to "KDP tools and resources." When you scroll down the page you will see that there are many dropdown menus for you to click on. The one you will be clicking on is going to be the first one that reads "Kindle Create." Once you've opened the drop-down menu, go ahead and download the Kindle Create software for either your Mac or Windows computer. When it has finished downloading, go ahead and open the program. You will now be able to upload your saved word document (a.k.a. your book). After it's been uploaded, you'll be able to see exactly how it will it will display on a tablet, phone, and kindle device. This is great because this preview will show you if you'll to change or adjust anything within your book. Finally, when you have finished reviewing your book and are happy with the result, click on the "Save as KDP File" button and return back to your kindle direct publishing dashboard where you were given the option to upload a paperback or kindle version of your book.

Go ahead and click on the option to add/upload your kindle eBook. Fill out all the required information about the book, the details, content, and the pricing. Once you're done simply press the submit button and upload your eBook onto to Amazon! It will take anywhere between 24 to 48 hours after pressing submit to have your book available on the market. I also highly recommend signing your book up for Kindle Unlimited. Kindle Unlimited is a subscription that allows its users to access a large selection of titles from the Kindle Store. You will be paid royalties every time someone "borrows" your book from the Kindle library.

Now that you have your eBook ready to go on the market, it's time you learn about Amazon's company CreateSpace. The great thing about self-publishing on Amazon and using CreateSpace is that you won't have to worry about the printing and shipping cost of your book. With CreateSpace you are able to upload and format your book to have it be printed and shipped in paperback form to your customers. What you'll need to do first is Google "CreateSpace." Go ahead and click on the first search result. You'll then want to sign up. Fill out all of the required information and submit your application. Once you've signed in, the "Member Dashboard" should be prompted up on your screen. Underneath the words "Member Dashboard" there should be a tab that says "My Projects," and to the left of it there should be a tab that says "Add New Title." Go ahead and click on "Add New Title."

There will be three things you'll need to fill out and do:
1. The title of your project (Your Book)
2. What kind of project it is (Paperback
3. Choosing a set up process (Click on Guided. You're not an expert *yet*)

Once you've uploaded your book, you'll need to choose a size for your paperback book. I usually go for 5" x 8" just because it makes the book size not too big or too small. It's perfect. You'll then be asked to review and proof your book either digitally or be given the option of buying a proof copy which will be sent to your address before you are able to publish it. I recommend going with the purchased copy because there's no other feeling than the one of seeing your book as a paperback for the first time. The benefit of this won't just be an emotional one, you'll actually be able to see what the finished product looks like. This will allow you to see any imperfections the book may have. Yes, this option will take about three business days longer than the instant digital proof, but it's better to get a paperback preview and fix any mistakes than approve your book and later find out in the reviews that it looks terrible.

    Now, keep in mind that the more books you publish the more streams of income you create. Your goal shouldn't just be to write a single book, your goal should be to publish upwards of fifteen books! Just follow the same process over and over and before you know it you'll be receiving royalties every month from every book you've written. Just make sure you focus on quality rather than quantity seeing as how some authors have more than 50 books on the market yet are making way less than some authors with only 15 books on the market.

Blogging

I'm sure you've heard about this method a number of times, but for good reason! Yes, this might sound generic and cliché, but I assure you it is nowhere near that. Blogging is actually one of the best ways you can make passive income. In fact, this is one of the best ways I've personally made passive income.

Okay, so how much money can you really make with a blog? Well, whether you're looking to create a stream of passive income or supplement your income with a little extra cash to pay for a few nice treats, you could definitely create a blog that will support your lifestyle. With a blog, you can pretty much make as much money as you would like from it. This is very true, but only if you are prepared to put in the hard work. That's right ladies and gentlemen. This isn't a get rich quick idea, but of course you already knew that.

There are a lot of great stories out there of very successful bloggers who have learned how to make money from blogging. For example, over the past couple of years, husband and wife, Bjork and Lindsay at PinchofYum.com, a food and recipe blog, have built up a huge following and have made nearly $25,000 every other month by simply blogging. Another blogging couple, Yeison and Samantha, who run mytanfeet.com are making over $5,000 per month while they travel the world and share their photos and stories on their blog. The money these people are pulling in every month sounds great, but I'm not going to lie to you, I wish this was something you could start one day and immediately be pulling in numbers like those couples. Creating a successful blog can take months, even years, before you start seeing a significant return on the time you've invested into starting it. Especially if you don't know how to monetize it correctly. But that is why I have created this book so that you can be confident in taking the right steps to achieving your blogging goals.

How To Start Blogging:

The first step you will take is probably the foundation to all of these ideas and one we have already talked about: finding the right niche. Yup. There is no point in starting a blog that you want to make money from without targeting a specific audience. There are thousands, even hundreds of niches out there. Some are broad and huge; some are small and virtually unknown. Some niches are easier to make money in than others. This is why your research is important. A good place to start when you are picking a niche is to look at your own interests in Google. For example, I launched a blog in the cryptocurrency niche last year which I then sold for a great profit. The reason I created that blog was because I enjoyed talking about crypto, learning about crypto, investing in crypto, etc. I also watched numerous videos and attended crypto conventions because I enjoyed it so much. I'm no expert, but it's something I liked and have created a very profitable blog around. The same goes for you. Once you've picked your preferred niche, it's time for the fun part; creating the blog itself.

There are a lot of good guides and articles out there on how to start a blog, but the first thing you'll need to do is purchase a domain for your website. I recommend using GoDaddy.com as your domain provider. The reason you'll need to purchase a domain is because you'll want to make your domain unique instead of the default branding domains websites will offer you. Once you have your domain ready, it's time to find a good hosting package site that will allow you to sign up and create your blog. Lucky for you I've already found the best hosting site.

Most site's might charge you upwards of ten to twenty dollars a month for their hosting package, but BlueHost.com offers many more options at a lower cost. They offer a $4.95 per month package option that I currently use which is fantastic. Feel free to go ahead and chose their more premium packages if you wish to do so, but I wouldn't recommend it if you're just starting out. Keep in mind after a few months of working on your blog, you could always upgrade to a better package. Now, why exactly are you buying a "package" from a "hosting" site? Well, the difference between a hosting site and a normal website creator, for example Wix, is that a hosting site allows your site/blog to be sponsored by ads. A normal website creator wouldn't allow you to do so.

After choosing their basic package, it's now time to insert your purchased domain from GoDaddy.com. Bluehost will ask you to either sign up with a new domain or sign up with one you already own. Simply type your domain in the "I have a domain" blank space and press next. You will then be asked to create your account by filling out the required information. After you've done that, you will be prompted to sign up for a 36-month term. What you'll want to do next is click on the drop-down menu and click on the 12-month term package option. I recommend doing this because it wouldn't be wise to commit to a three-year term if this is your first time creating a blog. Once you've submitted your information and have your site/blog up and running for edit, make sure you go ahead and install WordPress on your site. WordPress will allow you to format your site as a blog. After that, you'll either want to design the site to look visually appealing or hire someone off Fivver.com to do it for you at a very low price.

Like I've said, the most important thing here is you choose a specific niche that you can write a collection of posts around. This will attract readers and followers who will likely purchase a lot of your content. My niche is business, entrepreneurship, creating passive income and becoming financially free. (things that there will always be a demand for.)

Now that you have your blog up and running, it's almost time to start writing! But before you start pumping out post after post, make sure you set yourself of for future success by creating an email list. It's a more effective way to stay in touch with your audience and it makes it a lot easier to sell them books. Always give the option to sign up for your emailing list when writing your articles. Some sites, like BlueHost will offer widgets to install, like email capturing ones, that will appear on the screen of a viewer.

Things like Twitter, Facebook, and Instagram are also great ways to connect and build interest, but email is king. Especially when it comes to damage control. The servers for those sights could abruptly end out of nowhere or your account could be hacked/taken down at any moment. Not email. Emails are forever and your audience will tend to read them.

For example, a great way to persuade your audience to subscribe to your emailing list is to offer a free eBook. This is enough motive to make your audience sign up. After they sign up, you could either decide to email them the eBook or email them a link to a .pdf of your eBook. Another great way to have your audience sign up for your list will be a CTA (Call To Action). For those of you that are not familiar with a CTA, it basically calls the reader/audience to take action whether that be a button telling the reader to sign up for your emailing list to receive free valuable content or a button asking the reader to purchase your products. A CTA is very important when asking your audience to sign up for your list. I recommend either using mailchimp.com to create your email list or installing one of the many emailing list apps Bluehost has to offer.

You'll want to write several articles on your blog relevant to each of your published books. While most of your sales and your initial marketing efforts will be coming straight from Amazon, writing two or three articles on each book you publish will supply a nice flow of traffic towards your books. More importantly, it gives you something to write about. I've gotten to the point where all I need to do is publish one to two articles every month, but I try to make them super valuable and structure them so they sell a few books. You'll need to engage your readers to build a good relationship with them. This is one of my main focuses right now actually. My strategy is to email my list once or twice a week with valuable content or tips, so that the next time I release a book they trust me and know that it's likely to be valuable as well.

One of the many great advantages you have when creating a blog is that you are also able to create affiliate listings inside your articles and emails. For example, going back to affiliate marketing, when you signed up for your affiliate account, simply look up the affiliate link to your book(s) and insert a link to them inside of your articles and emails for your audience to click on. That way when your audience clicks on your link, doesn't buy your book, yet buys other products from Amazon within

24 hours of them clicking it, you'll also get a cut of that money. Isn't that awesome? This is what's known as "stacking." Stacking is when you are able to take trends/ideas and fuse them together to make a bigger idea that works in synergy. Use this method every time you get the chance in order to receive as many royalties as possible.

ATM Business

Now, I know what you're thinking, "I thought ATM's were only owned by banks?" Well, I'm here to tell you that this isn't true! I myself run an ATM business with the ATM's I've purchased. In fact, did you know that there are half a million automated teller machines (ATMs) currently in operation in the US as of 2015? While that number continues to grow every day and the convenience of being able to withdraw cash without having to go to the bank has attracted many people over the years, there is still plenty of good opportunities to be taken advantage of. Like I've already said, what may come as a surprise to most people is finding out that most ATMs are not owned by financial institutions (banks and credit unions). More than half of the ATMs in operation in the US today are owned and operated by independent ATM Deployers (IADs) or independent Sales Organizations (ISOs). While ISOs are typically larger organizations that pay large fees to be registered with networks, IADs can be anyone, from a single person (you) to a group of people. IADs typically invest their money in an ATM and generate income through it, or they help merchants and retailers manage their own ATMs and share the profits.

Now before we move into the steps of acquiring an ATM, I want you to understand how it is that you can create passive income from it. The name of the game when it comes to ATMs is recycling money. Think about it this way in the following scenario. Imagine someone is going to the barber shop to get their hair done. Once their hair has been cut and the person is ready to pay, the woman behind the cashier tells him that they only accept cash. This puts the person in a predicament because the only thing they probably have in their wallet is a debit or credit card. The lady then suggests the person use your ATM to withdraw some cash in order to pay. The person then walks over to your ATM and inserts their card. Before he is dispensed your cash, he has to agree to your surcharge of $2.00. The person presses okay and is given cash. Their account is then debited them amount that was taken out plus the surcharge. Within twenty-four hours, their bank will deposit the amount withdrawn and the surcharge into your account.

Basically, you put money into the ATM and people are willing to pay a fee in order to receive instant cash. After their withdrawal has been processed, this creates a debited fee of the cash they withdrew AND the additional surcharge fee of $2.00. Their bank then transfers both the withdrawn money and the fee from the person's account and deposits it into your account. Not only did you not lose any money, you actually made a profit! All you need to do now is keep filling the ATM with your money and wait for people to use it. Hence, recycling money. You make money every time the ATM is used.

Before we begin, it is important that I mention that this method will require some initial capital to begin with. The total amount of money that you will need will be between $3,000 to $5,000. Now, I know this may sound like a lot of money for some of you, but in the grand scheme of things $5,000 isn't a lot of money. In fact, I'm going to show you how you can do it for as little as $1,000.

Where To Start And What To Know In Order To Open An ATM Business:

Like every successful business does, you have to spot the gap in the market. Every entrepreneur is able to see potential where most only see a problem. The first thing you'll need to do is find a great location to place your ATM because location is king. I'm sure you'll be able to find locations near where you live, work, and hangout that can use an ATM. It could be a retail store, commercial building, festival, shopping center, arcade, adult store, gentlemen's club, nightclub, restaurants, manufacturing facility, event, or any place where people go. I will say the best places to place an ATM are inside or near those establishments that only accept cash as a payment. For example, certain eateries, stores, tattoo and piercing shops, and cannabis dispensaries. The key is to determine whether or not there is enough foot traffic in or near the establishment to make the ATM a profitable venture. The other opportunity is to find locations near you that already have ATMs in place, but where the equipment may be old and outdated, non-compliant, out of order, or owned and operated by someone else who is no longer keeping it maintained. This "gap" therefore becomes the location where you think an ATM is needed, the location wants a newer ATM, or where ownership of the store has changed.

Okay, like I said before, you will need some capital in order to start an ATM business. I did say that you will need between $3,000 and $5,000, but you could also start with only $1,000 instead. You could either choose to buy your ATM or lease it. There are many ATM companies out there that sell machines and lease machines, so it shouldn't be too difficult for you to find, select and lease one. A simple online search is all it takes for you to get in touch with a reputable ATM company. I personally use Best Products ATM Company (bpsands.com). *Not a paid advertisement* I'm not saying you have to go out and only buy from this company, but this is one of the best companies I have worked with. I ordered my first ATM from this company and have been happily working with them ever since. You can place an order for a machine, which will then be delivered to your home or any specified location that both parties have agreed on. This includes a specific date and time. Once you have the ATM machine in your possession, that's when the fun begins.

Now, for those that don't have $5,000 of capital to start with, you'll want to go online and search for a vender that will lease you a machine. A lot of the leases the ATM lenders are offering today are great deals, but keep in mind that the best way to make sure you'll be able to pay your monthly payment is by having the ATM used by people enough. This will all depend on the location of your ATM and the surcharge you have chosen. Remember, location is king!

"What about programming the ATM? Who will do that?" The ATM has to be programmed (or re-programmed if you buy a used model or take over the management of a previously installed one) for processing. Without the ATM processing, people will not be able to withdraw money from the ATM. In other words, it would be worthless. The great thing about Best Products is that before the ATM is delivered, they make sure to discuss with you the preferred denomination of the bills the ATM will be dispensing. Even if it's been two weeks after you've received your ATM and you have decided to experiment and change the denomination dispensed from the ATM because twenty-dollar bills are just too high, the company, Best Products, would be more than happy to walk you through reprogramming the ATM through the phone. Isn't that great? I think so and trust me it's been so great to be able to change the denomination of the bills dispensed when I've decided to change the location of my ATM to a different location. In some places it would be smarter to dispense $5 bills, like a barber shop for tips, rather than $20 bills for a bar or nightclub.

It is completely up to you with you wish to place the ATM on the outside or inside of an establishment. I recommend keeping your ATM inside due to weather conditions. Keep in mind that the ATMs are a bit on the heavier side so the option of bolting them to the floor wouldn't be a bad idea. If you don't have the proper tools to do it, or just don't know how to do it in general, the ATM company could send out a professional to install it for you. If you don't wish to pay someone else to install it, you can decide to unbox the ATM and bolt it to the floor yourself.

The next step will be to load the cash into your machine. You will need to have sufficient funds (cash) in your ATM for people to be able to withdraw the amount of money they'll need. Up until 2012, the average withdrawal transaction was $60. Now it's a little more. The average now, in 2018, is $80. That aside, you'll need to know the capacity of the ATM you purchased in terms of the amount of money it can hold. Most ATMs come standard with a 700 or 1,000 note cassette. Unless you have a really busy location, you won't necessarily have to fill the ATM up to capacity. The reality is that you can start with as little as 100 or so $20 bills and then use online reports and email reports to tell you when you need to add more cash into the cassette.

These steps illustrate how the ATM business works. You buy the ATM machine and set it up at a location of your choice where it is then available to the public to use. They can choose to withdraw money from their checking's, savings, or any other accounts associated with the card they use. Once the process of withdrawing is complete, you will receive a fee, the surcharge you've decided to implement, for each withdrawal transaction made on your ATM. This will be your revenue from the business. It is only a matter of time before your revenue increases to a point that your original investment is recouped and you start making a bigger profit. Keep in mind that this is the basic premise of how the ATM business works. There is a little more to this than simply buying a machine and installing it. You will have to complete the required banking paperwork, provide proper documentation, like your business EIN number from the IRS, and the basic background check. Don't let this discourage you. Running an ATM business may sound complex, but in reality, it's quite easy.

Okay, before you do anything else, you will need to obtain a business EIN. An Employer Identification Number (EIN) is also known as a Federal Tax Identification Number and is used to identify a business entity. Generally, almost all businesses need an EIN to function, but not all. You will definitely need one for your ATM business. You may apply for an EIN in various ways, and now you may apply online. The best and cheapest way to file for and obtain an EIN that I have found is through LegalZoom.com. I recommend filing for a DBA (Doing Business As) if you wish to not have any employees. Besides, you'll probably be the only one filling up the ATMs with your own money. Once your DBA registration is complete, you can open business bank accounts, write checks, and enter contracts. If you don't file a DBA and just start doing business under a different name you could face penalties and fines, not to mention the possibility of lawsuits. Sole proprietorships commonly use DBAs because a sole proprietorship's official, legal name is simply the name of the owner. A DBA lets them use a real business name.

    The next step after obtaining your EIN is to open a business checking's account at a bank. This part was the trickiest for me. I ended up going to many banks to ask if I could open a business account for my ATM business but was almost always rejected. The reason I was rejected was because the banks would use the excuse of "money laundering" to not allow me to set up anything with them. There were some banks that did allow me to open up a business account with my ATM business but had fees after a certain amount of ACH credit transactions every month. Be mindful of these fees. They add up. After weeks of trying to find the right bank I stumbled across a YouTube video that gave me the answers. The video was about two young men talking about their ATM business, and as they were loading one of their ATMs, I saw that the money bag they were using had a logo printed on it. The logo read "Bank of

America." That's when I closed out of app and drove straight to the nearest Bank of America with all my documents. When I arrived to the bank, I explained to them that I wanted to open a business account for my ATM business and they were more than happy to help me out. It was a great feeling after weeks of trying to find the right bank and being rejected. Persistence is key.

Now, as far as the background check goes, as long as you haven't committed a felony or a financial crime, you will most likely pass it. The reason the ATM company needs to run a background check before allowing you to purchase one of their ATMs is because you are basically wanting to become a small bank. You will be dealing with and dispensing money out to the public and will be receiving surcharges for your services. It's important to understand that although there may a lot of steps in the beginning, once you get the ball rolling there is not stopping it!

The last thing you'll need is an SLA (Site Location Agreement). Once you have verbal approval from the store or location owner to place your ATM, you'll need to obtain it in writing. No need to freak out here. The store owner probably wants to make the agreement binding and legal before you can install the machine in the store, too. This is where the SLA has to be completed. As the name suggests, the SLA is a document that lists the terms and conditions between the two parties, (e.g. you and the store owner). Though the agreement depends on the things agreed upon between you and the store owner, there is a standard format you can follow. It usually lists 15 to 20 clauses, each of them entailing to your machine being installed in the retail store. Most importantly, the SLA makes it clear that you are the owner of the ATM and the store is listed as the location. The other details your SLA include will be:

- Placement of machine
- Responsibilities to be borne by each party
- The length of time the agreement is valid for
- Insurance, maintenance, and other related issues

To put it simply, the SLA defines the roles and responsibilities for the store owner and the ATM machine operator (you). Make sure you discuss all of the details of the agreement in detail before signing on the dotted line.

Creating An Online Training Course/Program To Sell

It's no secret that the market for online courses is big and only growing. Research firm GM Insights valued online learning at $165 billion in 2015. By 2023, it could exceed $240 billion. That's a crazy amount of money. That being said, online courses are here, and they're here to stay. $240 billion by 2023, think about that. But how much can you really make with an online course? Take Graham Cochran for example, who teaches music production and pulls in up to $75K every month. Or Purna Duggirala, who back in 2014 made a cool million in a year. How? Teaching Excel. And yes, I run a 5-figure business selling courses, too. But it's not just about the big success stories. It's about the small wins, too. For example, you could easily create a course, and earn an extra $500 or $1000 a month. What would that mean to you?

But let's be real. It's going to take some work before you start making a single dollar. On the bright side you only have to create the course once and get paid over and over again. Often, you can even sell the same course for years. Now, I understand you may be thinking, "Who's going to buy my course if I'm not really an expert yet?" Don't worry about that. You don't need to be an expert to make a course just like we've previously discussed you don't need to be an expert to write a book.

How To Start Your Online Course:

As a course creator you have two options. Your first option is to actually already be the expert. If you already have a special skill or expertise, you can "be the expert" and share that knowledge. Let's say you're a certified massage therapist. Or you have an MBA in real estate. Or you're the Rock, Paper, Scissors world champion. In this case, sure, teach what you already know. But there's another option. You could be the curious novice you are and teach as you LEARN yourself! Here's what I mean: Choose a topic you're interested in, spend a weekend or two and read the 3 top-selling books on that topic, and BOOM. You are now enough of an expert. Meaning, you'll know more than 99% of people who are going to buy your course. Don't believe this is possible? Take Joseph Michael Nicoletti, who did just that. Joseph Michael Nicoletti teaches Scrivener. Joseph helps novelists write their novel with Scrivener and makes about $20,000 to $30,000 a month doing it. Let me rephrase that. He makes almost $1,000 a day by showing novelists how to use an app for writing. I know. Ridiculous.

When he decided to create an online course about Scrivener, he said, "I was just using it casually. I definitely wasn't an expert. I have never written a book or anything," and went on to say, "I purchased every book on Scrivener and studied everything I could find on it. I'd studied a particular feature, and then recorded a tutorial on it. Short 3-5-minute chunks mainly so it was easier for me to create, but it turned out to be one of the most popular features." Long story short, he created his course by learning one feature and filming a video about it. He then learned another feature and filmed another video on it. He created as he learned and went on to become a huge success.

This is why I love Michael's story: If you want to create an online course about something, anything, and you feel like "I don't know anything that I could teach" It only takes 5 letters… LEARN. And as you LEARN, document the process. This way you can create a course about almost anything that you're interested in. This can actually be an advantage for your course. Why? Because the teacher who knows the most is not always the best teacher. Experts sometimes skip over important information because it's too obvious to them. And what happens next? The student gets left behind. That's why a teacher who's just one step ahead of their students can sometimes create a more valuable course. Needless to say, you should always be honest about your experience and credentials. But the truth is you don't need to be the world's foremost expert to teach a course. Now, people are literally creating courses about every topic imaginable:

- Dating
- How to be a landlord
- How to fly a drone
- Watercolor painting
- Spiritual life coaching
- Copywriting
- Dog training
- And more...

The question is, what will you teach? Maybe it's already clear in your mind. Or maybe you're still looking for an idea. We have to make sure you choose a course idea that you are passionate about and can make money teaching it along the way. So, how do you make sure your idea is profitable? You don't want to spend time creating a course and then find out later on that no one wants to buy it. In fact, this is the biggest mistake new course creators make. They create a course, but they don't make sure students actually want to learn about the specific topic they chose. No wonder they struggle to attract students! But I've got you covered... The first lesson on choosing a profitable idea is to find out if someone has already created a course you want to create.

And if you do find out someone has already created a course, well then trust me, it's good news. I know that sounds counterintuitive but bear with me. When you come up with an online course idea that has never been done before, that means there's probably no one interested in buying it. Seriously. You might think, "But people need what I'm selling," and maybe they do. But the internet is so large that if people needed it, and were willing to buy it, there would have already been someone else selling it. As a matter of fact, if you come up with an idea for an online course, and you can't find someone else selling a course similar to what you want to offer, I'd find a new course. With that said, I have three strategies to help you come up with some profitable course ideas:

1. Take inventory of the things that people already ask you questions about or want your advice on.
2. If you're a freelancer or are already running a service business, take inventory of the things your clients struggle with the most and ask you questions about all the time.
3. Find the pain and eliminate it. This means going out into the real world and finding problems that people have. Then, you can create an online course that solves those problems.

Number three is my favorite strategy because it gets to the core of why people buy online courses. The short answer is people buy courses because they've got a problem and they want to solve it. Maybe they're looking to learn how to use a complicated piece of software. Maybe they don't fit into their favorite jeans and want to lose weight. Maybe they're stressed out and overwhelmed and want to take control of their calendar. Whatever the case may be, people buy online courses because they have a problem in their life and they want to solve it. Think about the problems your friends, colleagues, and family members come to you with. Listen to them and see if you can create a repeatable course that helps people solve problems. Sometimes it's an acute problem that people need to solve right away. For example, it could be a lingering problem. "How to be more confident," if you will. The more specific of a problem you solve, the easier it will be to sell your course.

The next step will be to test your idea. Test whether your course idea has potential by asking your friends and family. So how do you test it? There are two good ways that I've already used in the past. The first test would be to create a free mini email course. Here's what I mean... Instead of creating videos, worksheets, and additional resources, simply create a mini-course, and deliver it by email. You don't need a course website. You don't need some fancy software or design. Just deliver your course in email format. The best part? If you do this, you're not just validating your idea, you're also building up an email list of future students that will pay for another course at a later time.

Now, what if you could sell your course before you've created it? You can do just that by creating a sales page and asking people to "apply" to buy it. You could also put up a "Coming Soon" page that explains what the course will be. Send it out to your audience or run some Facebook ads and see if you can sell it. Both strategies, creating a mini email course and pre-selling your course, are easy ways to test your idea. Once you've tested your idea, the question is, "How do you create the actual course itself?

It's tough to create a multi-week course when you're doing this for the first time. There's a lot of content to create and you'll want your content to be top-notch. That's why the key to creating amazing course content is to start with a clear outline. Whether you're creating a free email course or your first paid course, here's what you absolutely need to remember: Start small. When people create online courses, they think they need to create some big, in-depth online course that covers everything they know, but that's a mistake. Don't do that. My first online course was made up of three little videos and a worksheet, and yet, it helped kick off my entire business. Just three little videos and some worksheets. Seriously. With that said, how do you decide what to cover in each lesson of your course? Well, that's why you need take make an outline. Just like making an outline for writing your book. Think of it as your course curriculum.

First, look at the problem your course solves. Then, ask yourself, "What are all of the steps people need to take to achieve this goal?" In other words, you're reverse engineering it. That's how you'll break your course down into individual lessons. After you break down your course into lessons, you will then have to do the same thing for each individual lesson. Finally, don't pack too much content into each lesson. Seriously. For a short course, lessons should be 5-10 minutes long. Definitely don't create lessons that are longer than 20 minutes. Otherwise students will often lose their focus, even if your delivery is great. What's great is now that you know the purpose of each lesson, creating the actual content becomes very straightforward. So, let's look at content creation in detail in the next step: Creating the course.

Most online courses are delivered in video format. Plus, they almost always include worksheets that help students implement what they've learned in the video lesson. Now, don't get too hung up on production quality. Instead, focus on teaching valuable content by giving insanely practical, step-by-step instructions. You do that and I guarantee your students will love your course. You can either record direct-to-camera videos or record a video of your screen as you go through the slides of a presentation. You don't need to hire a high-end videographer to shoot or edit your video lessons. You could simply use your phone to do both. There are many easy-to-use tools and software available. For screen recordings, you can try Camtasia. Or, if you're on a Mac, you can even use QuickTime for free. It's really simple. Because QuickTime is constantly updating and changing the layout, I recommend going onto YouTube and watching a quick five-minute tutorial on how to use QuickTime.

Let's talk briefly about worksheets. Worksheets should be .PDF files, so it's easy for people to download and print. Just create your document in Word or Pages. Then save it as a PDF and you're done. You can make your worksheets fillable. I do this in all my courses, but you don't have to.

The next step is getting your course online so you can start selling it! The good news is it used to be a real pain to get a course up and running. You had to upload your videos in one place, create a membership site, and then you had to coordinate everything with your email service, too. It was a mess, but not anymore! Today you don't need to be a tech-whiz to get your course up and running. Zippy Courses makes creating, and selling, your course a cinch. Needless to say, my own courses run on Zippy. With Zippy you can quickly and easily create your course page, protect your content, sell your course, and manage your students. I won't list all the features here, but you can read about some of the cool built-in tools that will help you make more course sales. With that said, you might be wondering, "Why do I need to create my own course site on Zippy as opposed to using a course platform, like Udemy or one of the many others anyway?" The answer? It comes down to control. With your own course site, you have total control over your course. Including price, design, students, a dedicated website (or a subdomain of your main website, like "course.yoursite.com"), and so on. Personally, I just don't like being at the mercy of one single company when it comes to my business. Also, I don't like sharing my revenue (Unless it's with hand-picked partners.) Which brings us to the final phase of building a successful online course business; Selling and promoting your course. The first decision is: How much will you charge?

For many new course creators, this is a tough decision. But when it comes to pricing, you must realize: People like buying courses – even when they can find the same information for free. It's counterintuitive, I know, but while people *could* find what you plan on selling elsewhere, they still have to find it. They also must figure out what information is legit and what information is junk, which most of the time free stuff can be. You usually get what you paid for. The alternative is often much easier, which is people usually find someone who created a course and they buy that. It's what I do, and it's what other people do, too. That's why the online course industry is exploding right now.

Time is one of the most valuable things we can never get back. Why waste time figuring out what's good or not when you can buy a course. Plus, paid courses also provide things that free information just can't: A proven structure that leads to results, dedicated student support, personal accountability, a community of like-minded students (this is huge), and so much more. If you've ever joined a high-quality course, you've likely experienced this yourself. So, don't undercharge when you sell your own course. To help you set a price, I suggest you use a very simple pricing rule. I call it the "Similar Outcome Approach." Here's how it works. Think of the ideal outcome of going through your course, and then ask yourself, "What would someone have to pay to get the same results with a different method?" You can compare it to other courses, software, hiring someone to do it, or hiring a coach. You should also consider the "cost of doing nothing" for your students.

Say you help someone clean up their diet, lose weight and live a much healthier life. What is that really worth? I'll tell you. A lot more than just thinking of your course as a collection of videos and PDFs. With that said, don't obsess over optimizing your price. In the beginning, just position it in the right price range. The table below should help you get started. Here's how I like to categorize it:

	A course that TELLS people what to do	A course that SHOWS people hot to do it	A course that SHOWS people how and provides dedicated SUPPORT
A course that solves a small problem	$0-$50	$50-$99	$97-$199
A course that solves a medium-sized problem	$100-$200	$200-$497	$497-$997
A course that solves a big, serious problem	$200-$500	$500-$997	$997-$3,997

The next step will be to get your course advertised to potential buyers. Remember, you don't want to build a course and then go looking for students. So, let's talk about how to do that. The best way to get students for your course is to offer it to your email list first. Why? Because email is still the easiest way to make sales online; especially if you already have a following from your blog, vlog and/or books. Send out an email that will offer the course to the subscribers first before it becomes available to the public at a slightly more expensive price. This will create a sense of urgency which will then incentivize people to buy it. Especially if you already have a loyal following that supports your content.

So... You've got your course. You're continuing to build your audience. Finally, it's time you launch your course! With that said, there are two ways you could launch your course. You would either continuously sell your course until an update/revision is required, or you could open the course up for a specific time period before closing it down for a while. Personally, I prefer to launch the open and close enrollment because most of my sales come from buyers that want in on the course before it closes for a while, but both options are viable.

If you're having trouble deciding which launch would be best to do, then think about this: Does your course solve an acute problem that people want and need a solution for right away? If so, it's often best to sell it continuously. For example, a course on "How to Use Macros in Excel." These buyers are people that likely need a solution NOW. If you make them wait too long for you to address the problem, you might miss out on some good reviews and present/future sales. On the flip side, does your course instead address a bigger, more complex problem? For courses that address lingering problems that people have been thinking about for months or years, like wanting to lose weight and gain muscle, an open and close launch would be great because you can build anticipation for buyers to sign up as soon as possible before the course itself closes. Makes sense?

Now, no matter how you sell your course, here is my 3-step course pitch formula. This simple formula takes people through three distinct phases of the sales process: Problem, Desire, and Solution. Here's how it works:

1. **Describe the PROBLEM:**

    Remember, your course solves a specific pain or problem. So, to kick of your launch, you need to remind people of the pain they're facing right now. Sounds negative, I know, but you need to show potential customers that you understand their problems and their struggles. By describing their pain in detail and reminding them of the cons, this will help you connect with potential buyers. Basically, you're telling your audience, "I understand. I feel your pain"

2. **Create DESIRE:**

Now it's time to create desire by showing the contrast between the situation as it is (step 1), and the situation that it could be. This is where you paint them the mental picture or actually visually show them of what their problem looks like resolved. Just make sure that you don't have mention your course just yet. You can use phrases like, "Wouldn't it be great if..." or "Picture yourself..."

3. **Pitch your SOLUTION:**

Here's where you bring up your course and set it up as the solution to their problem. The antidote, if you will. Tell them about your course, what's covered in it, and how it will help them resolve their problem or pain (as mentioned in step 1), and how this course will get them to where they want to be (As mentioned in step two). It's even better if you can SHOW people how it will help. For example, you could share a case study from a successful client or student that has completed your course.

My last advice is to keep learning how to progressively upgrade your courses. One of the best ways I've been able to do so is by reading other people's reviews on courses. I like to go onto YouTube and watch video reviews about other people's courses and see what people liked about them and what they didn't. This gives me the opportunity to implement what they did like into my own courses as well as implement a solution to the problems other courses had.

YouTube

So, can you make a living by making YouTube videos? Of course, you can. Let's meet YouTube's biggest millionaire: Felix Kjellberg, a.k.a. PewDiePie. A YouTube star with more than 60 million subscribers and almost 30 billion views who's also pulling in about $2,000,000 every month off YouTube ads. His videos are screech- and squirm-filled podcasts, in which he plays video games and does meme reviews for his audience. The overwhelming popularity of this YouTuber is attributed to his ability to build a close relationship with his audience, without technicalities or formalities getting in the way.

So where to begin? First things first. Let's create a YouTube account and set up your channel. Head over to YouTube.com and click "Sign In" in the upper right corner of the screen. Once you've clicked it, I encourage you to sign up with a Gmail account (Google Mail), if you haven't already done so. Once you've signed up for the account, go back to the home page by clicking on the YouTube logo on the upper right-hand side of the screen. Once you are back to the home screen, in the upper right-hand side of the screen where the "Sign in" button used to be, there will now be a colored circle with a letter on it.

Typically, the letter will be based on your email or the first letter of your name. Go ahead and click on that colored circle. A drop-down menu will then appear and what you'll need to do next is go down to "My Channel" and click on it. This will take you to the section of your channel where you can optimize and customize your YouTube channel. Once you're done with that, click on the video camera icon with the little plus sign in the middle of it in order to upload a video or go live. Once you've clicked on "Upload Video" you will arrive to a screen where you will be given the option to upload a video from your phone or computer. Once you have finished uploading your video, simply add a little bit of text to your description talking about your product or products and leave your affiliate link in the description as well. The key here is to push out as much content directly correlated to product reviews and product comparisons in order to create a successful passive stream of income. A channel is like your personal presence on YouTube.

In addition, whenever you create a YouTube account, you will be given access to other Google products and tools such as Gmail and Google Drive. When you create your channel, remember to navigate to the advanced option and key in relevant keywords to your video content under Channel Settings. It will be easier for people and Google to locate you whenever your keywords are relevant to your videos. Try to use a short and easy username too if possible. If you want to use an existing account, you can change your username by editing it on your Google+ account.

Next, you'll want to create your video content. Depending on what kind of videos you want to upload, your videos can be both long and short. More importantly, go for high-quality video content. People will leave and stop watching your video if the quality is blurry, so it'd be very wise to invest in a good quality camera if you don't already own one.

Now, when it comes to uploading videos, here are some effective and helpful tips I have for you:

- It's alright if you're not doing it right the first time. You just need to try more, practice more, upload more and you can become better at it. Practice makes perfect.
- Always aim to improve your content by investing into tools such as a better camera, a drone, a tripod, a monopod, get a friend to hold your camera or using a gimbal.
- Learn to use software and programs to enhance the quality of your videos. Sometimes you need to add subtitles if you're doing the commentary, and sometimes you need to make your video pictures brighter and/or add in a watermark.

Building your own audience through a YouTube channel is like building a blog. Your content is your videos and you must be consistent with uploading them. Try to stick to a regular and consistent publishing schedule if possible. People will be more likely to subscribe to your channel when you are consistent enough because they will be expecting something fresh and new from you. You don't have to upload everyday either. You could start uploading once a week and progressively upload more times per week. Maybe even getting to the point of uploading daily like a lot of channels do. Make sure you tag and describe your video content with relevant keywords. Make sure people understand your description and know what you are trying to present to them. If your keywords are good and relevant, chances are that people may find your videos through YouTube searches.

When it comes to making money from YouTube, there is no way to get around building an audience and gaining traffic or views to your videos. You must learn to market and promote your videos. There is no point to create a good quality video that you think people will love, but only to find that there are no people to watch it. Remember who your target audience is and understand what they want. If you are trying to target an audience who is looking for entertainment, make your videos interesting and share-worthy. Keep uploading video content and get people to love your productions. Don't forget to share your videos to other social media such as

Twitter and Facebook. If you don't want to share your own video, nobody will distribute your videos elsewhere on the internet.

Whenever other people do eventually share your videos without having to pay for ads, which is called organic marketing, you will get the additional views and marketing you want. This is especially true when other authority figures or websites grab your videos and share them with their fans. You will see a huge traffic increase and this is what you want. You'll also always want to interact with your viewers. Reply to their comments whenever possible and build a relationship from there. One of the ways PewDiepie was able to get such a huge following was due to him replying to other people's comments and interacted with his audience from time to time.

Now that your videos have been uploaded, it's time to monetize your videos. In order to earn the advertising revenue from your videos, you must first enable the monetization option. This simply means that you allow YouTube to place and show ads on your videos. Whenever someone watches an ad, you will get paid.

First, log in to your YouTube account and go to "My Channel." Then, go to "Video Manager" on the top. Next, click your channel and choose "Enable Monetization." Afterwards, you'll start to monetize your videos once the "Monetize with Ads" box has been checked. Once it's been checked, in order to monetize a specific video, one you've already uploaded, just open your "Video Manager," click on the "$" sign on the video you want to monetize, and then check the box. The YouTube advertisement functionality is the same as AdSense. If you already have an AdSense account, you can link it with your YouTube account. If you don't already have an AdSense account you'll want to set that up. Your payment will come through AdSense. Simply go to Google and search "AdSense" and click on the first result. Once at the home page, click "Create Account" and follow each step until your account is ready to go.

After you've uploaded your videos, shared them, and monetized them, you'll want to know how they perform. You can do this by checking their performance through analytics. In your "Channel" menu, just click and go to Analytics. You can see the estimated earnings, ad performance, video views, demographics and more. You'll want to use the information available to you to better understand your audience and how you can improve your future video content.

The key here is to create video content that will resonate with your viewers. When your viewers like your content, they will share it and recommend it to their friends either through YouTube itself or posted it somewhere in other social media like Facebook and Twitter. This will generate a lot more views. The more views you receive, the more times ads will play on in your videos. The more ads play, the more revenue you'll receive.

One of the best things about creating a YouTube channels is that you'll be able to tap into multiple streams of income through it. Although making money from YouTube advertising can be hard at first, there will be other ways to receive revenue during that initial hump. There are many other methods on how you can earn money through your YouTube videos and not just through advertising. Below are some great examples:

1. **Become an affiliate and sell through YouTube:**

    Do you know that YouTube is just a platform or a medium that you can get traffic from? You can promote other people's products through your YouTube videos. It is challenging to get a million views, and sometimes, the advertisement revenue from YouTube can be low. Things will be different when you sell affiliate products. What you need is a targeted audience to watch your videos. For example, you can earn $50 from an affiliate sale with just 500 views of your video. This is how I make the most money through affiliate sales.

2. **Getting Sponsorships:**

Have you ever seen a sponsored article in blogs? You can do the same with YouTube videos. When you've built up your own audience, you can sell sponsorships or airtime directly from advertisers. The good news about selling sponsorship is that you do not have to give YouTube a cut and you can negotiate the fee that you desire.

3. **Transition into Speaking Engagements:**

When you become good enough and you achieve certain popularity/credibility in your industry, people will approach you and request that you speak or perform for them. For a fee, of course. Usually, this will only happen when your YouTube channel is focused on a very specific niche or type of audience. When you become good at it and gain reputation, people will look for you and hire you for speaking engagements.

4. **Selling Your Expertise:**

Sell a course! For example, once you've build a strong audience through your channel, people may want a more personal and advanced version of your channel. That will be your opportunity to sell your expertise and make money from premium videos or coaching. This technique is extremely popular in the information industry. People are willing to pay to learn how to use Photoshop, how to cook, how to bake a delicious chocolate cake, how to train their parrots, how to build a website, etc.

Patience Is Key

The one thing that hurts entrepreneurs the most is their lack of patience. One thing I'm sure of in this world is that nothing of value comes easily. In fact, anything of value takes time, whether it's a matter of developing a skill, building a brand, launching a business, or creating passive income. Although entrepreneurs like myself like to simplify matters as much as possible, the truth is that the world is a complex place, full of nuance. These things take time.

There are no shortcuts, so there's no reason to feel rushed. I get it though, you want to be successful now, but that's not how it works. If you continue to have this rushed mentality, the only thing you will be doing is causing harm to your wellbeing. It will constantly feel like you are stuck in the mud and not going anywhere. You will begin to feel the weight of the world on your shoulders and slowly sink into a black abyss of depression. Shortly after that, all this negative energy will leak into the rest of your life and you will quit. Do not set yourself up for this trap. Why do you need that new house or car this very instance? Too many of us fall under this sort of thought process where we ask and wonder if I put in all this work, then what's in it for me right now. This isn't a 100-meter dash nor is it your typical 5k. This is much greater than that. Your journey is much greater than that.

As entrepreneurs, we live in a world that values quick thinking and dynamic action. This is not a bad thing in and of itself. However, when you allow these traits to manifest in the form of impatience, problems arise. As difficult as it may be, entrepreneurs must remember that patience, especially in business, truly is a virtue.

In the far east they have something that's called the Chinese bamboo tree. The Chinese bamboo tree takes five years to grow. They have to water and fertilize the ground where it is every day, and it doesn't break through the ground until the fifth year. But once it breaks through the ground, within five weeks it grows 90 feet tall.

Now, the question is does it grow 90 feet tall in five weeks, or five years? The answer is obvious. It grows 90 feet tall in five years. Because at any time, had that person stopped watering and nurturing and fertilizing that dream, that bamboo tree would've died in the ground. Great things take time to grow.

Do me a favor

Thank you for purchasing this book and supporting me. I'm confident you're well on your way to accomplish great things and gain your freedom through passive income. Please gift this book to everyone you think needs to read it. Please take a moment to write a great review on Amazon. Reviews are the best way for independent authors like myself to get noticed and sell more books. I also read every review and use the feedback to write future revisions and future books.

Thank you from the bottom of my heart.

Other books:
The Millionaire In Progress:
How To Really Become Financially Free

www.ingramcontent.com/pod-product-compliance
Lightning Source LLC
Chambersburg PA
CBHW020449220526
45464CB00002B/922